"NOTHING IS NOW
TO BE HEARD OF
IN CONVERSATION,
BUT THE BALLS,
THE FOX-HUNTS,
THE FINE ENTERTAINMENTS,
AND THE GOOD FELLOWSHIP,
WHICH ARE TO BE
EXHIBITED AT THE
APPROACHING CHRISTMAS."

Philip Vickers Fithian
Saturday, December 18, 1773

Discover Yuletide
at Winterthur

by Deborah V. R. Harper

Table of Contents

The Spirit of Yuletides Past

*I*magine . . .

. . . a bustling market square on Christmas Eve, the cobblestones reverberating with the cries of street vendors hawking their wares and turkeys squawking at the butcher's stall, while in the lantern light enticing trinkets—potential gifts—gleam on the tin-peddler's bench, and snow sparkles on the ground.

. . . the lively notes of a Virginia Reel, the ladies' silken gowns gleaming in the candlelight, as servants step skillfully between the dancers, balancing trays of oyster loaves and frothy syllabubs.

. . . twilight, a voice chanting the words of an ancient Hebrew blessing, and the steady glow of the *shammash* as it imparts its flame to eight candles of remembrance.

. . . a scruffy newsboy, hat in hand, shuffling into an elegant town home on New Year's Day, hopeful of receiving a coin or two in token of his service.

. . . a riot of ribbons dangling from a chandelier, flying off to the top of the chimneypiece and under the chairs, each strand bearing at intervals well-chosen gifts for fortunate recipients, while in the corner, toys tumble out from under a tree bedecked with candles, banners, glass beads, and candy.

These are but a few of the scenes that have delighted visitors to Yuletide at Winterthur in recent years. This seasonal tour through twenty of the museum's famous period rooms, each specially decorated for the

Holiday Shopping

Early Christmas shoppers were often tempted by the wealth of possibilities offered by merchants, street vendors, and itinerant peddlers in the cities and market squares. One man noted in 1869 that he hoped to spend not more than twenty dollars but was "inflamed by a pretty cameo brooch, and moved much to the extent of $200."

Left: Rococo Revival Parlor.

2

The YOUNG SWEEP giving BETTY her CHRISTMAS BOX

The Kissing Ball

Greens were used sparingly in domestic settings before the mid-1800s. In this late eighteenth-century print, *The Young Sweep Giving Betty Her Christmas Box*, the ever-present kissing ball is augmented by sprigs tucked into the pot lids and candle cups.

holiday season, has been an annual offering at Winterthur since 1978, when the first organized Yuletide tour was presented to the public. For the last twenty years, ongoing research into the origins of our modern holiday celebrations has revealed that the customs enjoyed by our ancestors were often strikingly different from what we know today. Current popular culture promotes an ideal of the holiday season that is child centered and celebrated with family gatherings, church attendance, and goodwill toward all. Two hundred years ago, however, the holiday season was adult centered; it elevated New Year's Day over Christmas, divided people along class lines, and was often given over to such mischief and mayhem that many churches and individuals actively disassociated themselves from it. How and why did our perceptions of the holiday season change so dramatically? The Yuletide tour considers these issues while it reveals some of the origins of our modern holiday traditions.

Visitors on the Yuletide tour are often surprised by what they see, for the displays strive to evoke a holiday season that early Americans would have recognized, not one that reinforces today's romantic fantasies and misconceptions about the past. Thus, they do

3

not find Christmas trees in every room or an abundant use of evergreen decorations, for neither were commonly seen in domestic settings before the mid-1800s. Instead, loosely gathered "kissing balls" dangle from chandeliers, and sprigs of boxwood garnish picture frames and candle cups. There are no wreaths or sprays of fruit and foliage ornament-

ing doors and windows as this type of decoration is a more recent innovation. In the past, elaborate table settings were considered sufficient decoration for any occasion, and colorful fruits, rare and expensive in the wintertime, were piled into towering pyramids meant to delight the palate as well as the eye. Most important, many of the entertainments depicted on the Yuletide tour have nothing inherent to associate them with Christmas because for a large percentage of the population, Christmas did not figure into the season's celebrations.

A Sumptuous Display

For many people, fresh fruit in the wintertime was an expensive indulgence. Hostesses might show it off by creating beautiful displays, including high pyramids garnished with greenery.

4

Christmas in the Colonies

Kershner Kitchen and Kershner Parlor

Holiday preparations meant that a great deal of time was spent in the kitchen. Hannah Burton noted in her diary on December 23, 1813, "We had 30 pies made by half past 8 in the morning."

Left: Marlboro Room.

wo centuries ago, December and January were regarded as the social high point of the year, but not because of Christmas or even New Year's celebrations. Social engagements filled the winter calendar simply because in an agrarian society, winter was when people had enough freedom from farming to devote themselves to parties and visits, perhaps even to be away from home for several days at a time. It was also cheaper and more efficient to butcher animals in the fall than to feed them expensive grain over the winter months, so this was the time of year that people enjoyed fresh meat dressed with fresh vegetables from the recent harvests. This combination of factors determined that winter would be a time of socializing and eager consumption.

Because this season was often marked by gluttonous overindulgence, excessive drinking, and raucous behavior, many religious leaders in America urged their followers to refrain from tarnishing the name of the Lord by using his birth as an excuse for such displays of excess. Protest against unseemly Christmas revelry was especially strong in New England, where the Puritans had maintained a strong presence since their early colonization there. The Puritans denounced Christmas revelry as impious and unsanctioned by Scripture. While they praised God for the birth of his son as recorded in the Gospel of Luke, they knew that the Bible is unclear as to its precise date. How then could

6

Nativity Scene

Scenes from the Bible, such as the one on this appliqued picture, are not commonly depicted on objects made in early America, where they were met with strong disapproval by the dominant Protestant ideologies.

a single day be set aside to celebrate it? As the Reverend Ezra Stiles, Congregationalist minister and later president of Yale, noted in 1776, "Tho' it had been the will of Christ that the anniversary of his birth should have been celebrated, he would at least have let us known the day." The Puritans knew well that the early church fathers had borrowed the old Roman festival of Saturnalia, a pagan celebration that marked the winter solstice, and had given it an overlay of Christian significance as a way to win converts. The gluttony and immorality that marked observances of the Lord's birth in England was intolerable to the Puritans, and they determined that it would find no place in America.

Efforts to control Christmas excess began immediately upon arrival in Massachusetts. In 1620, just a few weeks after landing at Plymouth, Gov. William Bradford noted with satisfaction that on Christmas Day "no man rested." The following year, some free-spirited individuals were found observing Christmas with "gaming [and] reveling in the streets," but Bradford quickly brought an end to their carousing. He stated that although it might go against their consciences to work on the twenty-fifth of December, it went against *his* conscience to see them pass the day in idleness. His position was strengthened in 1659 when a law was passed in the Massachusetts Bay Colony charging a fine of five shillings to anyone who stopped work or feasted on

Christmas Day. Forced in 1681 to repeal the law, the Puritan leaders nevertheless continued trying to impress their position upon their followers.

Without the force of law behind them, church leaders had a hard position to sell, especially after the first Anglican and Huguenot churches were established in New England in the mid-1680s. These denominations did not oppose Christmas observances. In 1698 diarist Samuel Sewell noted the difficulty of trying to win people over to his position: "This day I speak with Mr. Newman about his partaking with the French Church on the 25. December on account of its being Christmas-day, as they abusively call it. He stoutly defended the Holy-days and the Church of England." In 1703 he was still grumbling and noted, "The Christmas keepers had a pleasant day. Governor and Mrs. Dudley at church, and Mr. Dudley made a pretty large entertainment after." In 1711 the Reverend Cotton Mather lamented when he learned that "a Number of young people of both sexes, belonging, many of them, to my Flock, had on Christmas night, this last week, a Frolick, a revelling Feast, and Ball." Although the Puritan leaders were sorely challenged to keep their flocks on the narrow path, references to Christmas celebrations in New England remained infrequent for many years, indicating that Puritan influence remained strong.

In marked contrast to events in New England, the southern colonies were settled largely by Anglicans, who did not oppose Christmas observance. Settlers at Jamestown,

The Reverend Cotton Mather

A talented preacher and a renowned theologian, Mather (1663–1728) was also a determined historian who recorded the great achievements of the Puritan fathers of New England. His steadfast opposition to Christmas frivolity was one example of his "defense of our invaded churches."

Southern Hospitality

Southern hospitality permitted many festive gatherings during the holiday season, such as is depicted in this informal sketch drawn by a member of the party.

Time to Dance

Dancing was an integral part of many early festivities. Diarist Philip Vickers Fithian wrote in 1774, "Virginians are of genuine Blood—They will dance or die!"

Virginia, in 1608 strove to "keep Christmas with feasting and merriment" and thereby set a pattern that continued in the South. This is not to suggest that unfettered revelry ruled the day. *The Virginia Gazette* in 1739 denounced extremes on both sides, noting, "Tis ridiculous to do nothing but fast and mortify all Christmas, and to keep a Monkish holiday, as it is to banquet and carouse alonge, and make a Bacchanalian Time of it." Responsible Anglicans typically observed Christmas Day with a morning church service and perhaps an especially good meal afterward but little more. As Englishman Nicholas Cresswell, travelling in Virginia in the 1770s, noted in his journal, the holiday was "very little observed in this country."

The winter *season,* however, was a time for liberal drinking, eating, visiting, and dancing. Philip Vickers Fithian, tutor to a wealthy plantation family on the Northern Neck of Virginia, provided detailed accounts of "the Balls, the Fox-hunts, the fine entertainments and the good fellowship" enjoyed during the holiday season, which was "to continue til twelfth-day."

In the Middle Colonies, as in Virginia and the South, religious persuasion played a large part in determining how people kept Christmas. The earliest reference to a Christmas tree in America comes from the diaries kept by the Moravian Church of Bethlehem, Pennsylvania, which document the custom of decorating wood pyramids with evergreens. The Christmas Day 1747 entry records:

> We provided for a happy occasion for the children. . . several small pyramids and one large pyramid of green brushwood had been prepared, all decorated with candles and the large one with apples and pretty verses.

Also in Pennsylvania, Swedish traveler Peter Kalm contrasted Anglican practices with those of Quakers in Philadelphia in 1758: "I heard several members of the English Church wish one another a happy Christmas holiday. In the English Church a sermon was preached in the morning; but . . . the Quakers paid not the slightest attention to Christmas; carpentry work, blacksmithing, and other trades were plied on this day just as on other days." Philadelphia Quaker Elizabeth Drinker reinforced Kalm's observations in her diary some forty years later: "December 25, 1796. Called Christmas Day. Many attend religiously to this day; others spend it in riot and dissipation. We, as a people, make no more account of it than any other day."

Accounts such as these indicate that throughout the colonial period, controversy reigned over whether and how people should celebrate Christmas. By the time of the nation's centennial in 1876, however, that situation had changed dramatically.

Moravian Pyramid Tree

This modern Moravian pyramid tree was derived from the 1790s print above, probably made in Germany.

In the first quarter of the 1800s, the most obvious symbol of Christmas, the decorated tree, was evidenced only in a few references from areas of Germanic settlement. By 1890, however, Christmas was a legal holiday in all states and territories, and the iconography of Christmas that we recognize today—trees, greens, gifts, and Santa Claus—was thoroughly ingrained in American popular culture. Many factors contributed to this transformation. The urbanization and increased mobility of American society fostered the dissemination of new ideas throughout the broader population. Much of what we now think of as "old-fashioned" or "traditional" about Christmas was then new. At the same time, the rapid industrialization and expansion of the consumer market brought vast quantities of manufactured goods within reach of large segments of society. The proliferation of mass-market periodicals and books provided an advertising venue for manufacturers and merchants as well as a forum for authors whose sentimentalized accounts of fictitious holiday celebrations created a popular image of Christmas "as it should be."

The antebellum period was an age of reform in America, and most reformers found something in Christmas that could serve their cause. For nineteenth-century reformers, Christmas as it should be was very different from Christmas as they knew it. Throughout

Smart Dolls and Other Whimsies

English journalist Harriet Martineau described a tree in 1835: "Smart dolls and other whimsies glittered in the evergreen. . . . We were all engaged . . . in filling the gilded egg-cups and gay paper cornucopias with comfits, lozenges, and barley-sugar."

Left: A tabletop tree decorated with dolls, edible treats, and handmade ornaments.

12

Christmas Morning
By the early 1800s, shopkeepers advertised an array of toys suitable to give to children for Christmas.

the colonial period, Christmas observances generally were public events. Some were church services, of course, but many were public displays of rowdy, possibly violent, and often immoral behavior. In the nineteenth century, however, Christmas was domesticated.

Reformers created an ideology of Christmas that emphasized benevolence and charity toward the less fortunate as well as strong family bonds. Central to this "taming" of Christmas was its transformation from a time when *adults* would engage in raucous frivolity to a time when *children* were the focus of attention. This new attitude toward Christmas both resulted from and continued to help foster the idealization of the family as a sacred entity. It was an era when children were seen as innocents who needed to be sheltered from evil influences outside the home. Thus the oft-reproduced image of adults and children gathered in a closed circle around a Christmas tree is an accurate real-

ization of the values that nineteenth-century society held dear.

It is just such a scene that is depicted in one of the earliest images of a Christmas tree in America. In a sketch dating from about 1812, Pennsylvania German artist John Lewis Krimmel recorded a family group of adults and children gathered around a Christmas tree. Typically, the trees in the antebellum period were of the tabletop variety, the earliest ones being some type of broadleaf evergreen, simply decorated with edible treats. Often, an array of miniature houses and figures surrounded the base of the tree. The earliest Christmas trees were found in regions where large numbers of Germans had settled, but by the 1830s they were documented in other areas as well. In Boston, for example, followers of radical abolitionist

O Christmas Tree

In this sketch, by John Lewis Krimmel, of a Pennsylvania German Christmas, cookies decorate the tree, and plates of goodies are prepared for the children.

14

Made in Germany

This tree features a collection of embossed paper ornaments known as Dresdens. Made in Germany in the late 1800s, they are among the most prized of early tree decorations.

William Lloyd Garrison displayed decorated trees at the annual antislavery fairs they sponsored to support their cause. About the same time, women's groups began sponsoring Christmas fairs to raise money for churches, orphanages, and other charitable endeavors; at some of these, patrons were charged a small fee to see a decorated Christmas tree.

Such public displays helped popularize the Christmas tree by introducing it to a wide audience. The same effect resulted from illustrations of trees in popular periodicals. The most famous of these appeared in the December 1850 issue of *Godey's Lady's Book*. The image shows a family—father, mother, and children—grouped around a table that holds a decorated fir tree. Supposedly intended to represent an American family, the illustration was actually copied from an image that had appeared two years earlier in the

Illustrated London News showing Queen Victoria, Prince Albert, and their children around a tree at Windsor Castle. For those who had not seen it the first time, *Godey's* reprinted the image in 1860.

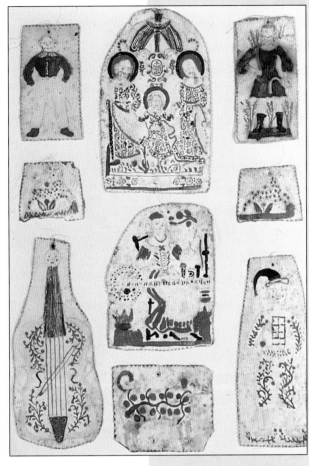

Alongside the illustrations of decorated trees that appeared in popular magazines were sentimental stories that created a common Christmas "experience" for readers. Throughout the nineteenth century, Christmas was popularized through the writings of famous authors such as Washington Irving, Clement Moore, and Charles Dickens; their influence was profound. The "right jolly old elf" that Moore described in his famous poem, "A Visit from St. Nicholas," still reigns as America's benevolent gift-giver almost two centuries later. Charles Dickens's *Christmas Carol,* with its emphasis on family unity and love and charity toward those less fortunate, meshed perfectly with the ideals of the age and remains the classic story of Christian redemption.

Relics of Christmas Past

Made of almond paste and sugar, marzipan tree ornaments often were given to the children to eat. Some thrifty housewives, however, made their decorations out of wheat flour and glue, so that they might be saved from year to year.

ince the late 1800s, much of the excitement generated by the holiday season has centered on Christmas, but prior to that time, other holidays took precedence. New Year's Day long reigned as the high point of the winter festivities. Even during times when Christmas observances received almost unremitting criticism, attitudes toward New Year's Day celebrations were more lenient. Samuel Sewell, whose diary is filled with resentful accounts of his forty-year struggle against Christmas-keeping in Boston, over the same period records several occasions when he was a full participant in New Year's festivities. Throughout the colonial and early national periods, New Year's was the popular day for gift exchanges, and on January 1, 1720, Sewell noted, "Gave Col. Dyer one of Mr. Foxcroft's books. Just before Prayer in the morning, Mr. Cooper sends my wife a Present of Oranges and a Shattuck; and to my daughter Judith, a Stone-Ring and a fan." Other times he records giving money to the trumpeters on the Common who heralded the New Year at first light.

Welcoming the New Year with trumpet blasts, gunfire, and other raucous behavior was common throughout early America—a remnant of the primitive belief that evil spirits and demons were rampant at the turning of the year but might be scared off by loud noises. The New Year's shoot was a popular group activity in rural German communities in Pennsylvania. Young men assembled

Holiday Merrymaking

Prints such as William Hogarth's *A Midnight Modern Conversation* illustrate the carousing that was a frequent component of early holiday festivities.

Left: Shooting in the New Year.

in groups of as many as fifty and made the rounds from farm to farm, firing guns and creating general pandemonium. At each farm the men might expect to be invited into the house for food and drink. The New Year's shoot also occurred in cities, but tolerance there was low. Many people objected to the mischief, noise, and drunkenness that accompanied the festivities. On December 31, 1793, Elizabeth Drinker observed, "They are now practicing the foolish custom of firing out the old year; may the next be spent to good purpose by those who are spared to see the end of it."

New Year's historically was the highlight of the winter social season, and visiting others was the primary social activity. Visits might be informal or highly structured. The "shooting in" of the new year was one form of structured visiting. A closely related practice was "mumming," which is defined as disguising, or masking, oneself. The mummers, like the shooters, were groups of young men who went from house to house, but they tended to operate in urban settings. Disguised, the men demanded entry into homes and, once admitted, would perform a short play. They expected some remittance for the entertainment they provided and were inclined to do mischief if they were refused entry to a house or if their remuneration was not forthcoming. Samuel Breck of Boston described a visit from the mummers in the late 1700s:

> They were a set of the lowest blackguards, who, disguised in filthy clothes and oft-

times with masked faces, went from house to house in large companies, and, bon gré, mal gré, obtruding themselves everywhere, particularly into the rooms that were occupied by parties of ladies and gentlemen, would demean themselves with great insolence. I have seen them at my father's, when his assembled friends were at cards, take possession of a table, seat themselves on rich furniture and proceed to handle the cards, to the great annoyance of the company. The only way to get rid of them was to give them money, and listen patiently to a foolish dialogue between two or more of them. . . . In this way they would continue for half an hour; and it happened not infrequently that the house would be filled by another gang when these had departed. There was no refusing admittance. Custom had licensed these vagabonds to enter even by force any place they chose.

Because of the violence and disrespect for authority that often resulted, mumming was banned in some cities in the mid-1800s. Working-class youth objected to having their entertainment abolished by the cultural elites, however, and would not give up the practice. A compromise allowed mumming to be reintroduced under controlled circumstances and with established lines of authority. Thus mumming continues today in parade format, notably at the annual New Year's Day Mummers Parade in Philadelphia and at Mardi Gras in New Orleans.

New Year's Calling with the du Ponts

New Year's calling remained an active tradition for the du Ponts in Delaware. Ruth Wales du Pont, wife of museum founder Henry Francis du Pont, greeted callers in the Port Royal Parlor with cake, cookies, coffee, and hot mulled wine. Some years, as many as thirty cakes were consumed.

A more genteel form of structured visiting was the New Year's calling, which took place in cities, especially New York, in the first half of the nineteenth century. Supposedly introduced by Dutch settlers, the practice became widespread when large numbers of French émigrés settled in New York in the aftermath of the French Revolution. On January 1, women remained at home while men spent the day paying visits to, or calling on, all their female acquaintances. Julia Ward Howe described the practice in her *Reminiscences:*

> In every house of any pretension, the ladies of the family sat in their drawing rooms, arrayed in their best dresses, and the gentlemen of their acquaintance made short visits, during which wine and rich cakes were offered them. It was allowable to call as early as ten o'clock in the morning. The visitor sometimes did little more than appear and disappear, hastily muttering something about "the compliments of the season." The gentlemen prided themselves upon the number of visits paid, the ladies upon the number received.

For the women who received callers, preparing the special libations and "rich cakes" to be offered to the gentlemen no doubt added many hours of work to their holiday preparations; but at least on the day itself they remained comfortable in their houses. For the men, New Year's Day brought the challenge of hurrying through the cold and the snow to fulfill their social obligations. Adam Hodgson described the calling from a man's perspective:

> I had an opportunity, on New Year's Day, of witnessing and joining in the old Dutch custom of running the round of complimentary calls, immediately after church. We must literally run, if we have tolerably extensive acquaintances, for we call on every lady we know. . . . It is quite ridiculous to see the crowds in the streets, all urging their rapid course, as if they were couriers on important business, and looking eagerly at their lists, to see that they made no omissions. They stay only two or three minutes at a place, sometimes not even sitting down; and in several instances, the lady of the house told me she did not know the parties who had just retired.

Although Hodgson was unaware of it, his account of a New Year's calling in New York in the 1820s foretold the custom's imminent demise. The challenges he faced making his rounds became insurmountable as the city grew in size during the ensuing decades. In addition, the problem of strangers intruding upon the festivities—"the lady of the house told me she did not know the parties who had just retired"—increased apace. As Julia Ward Howe described it,

> A number of young men of the city took it upon themselves to call in squads at

houses which they had no right to molest, consuming the refreshments provided for other guests, and making themselves disagreeable in various ways. This offense against good manners led to the discontinuance . . . of the calling.

Although the participants would probably disagree, the genteel custom described by Howe and Hodgson actually had much in common with the rustic New Year's shoot and the mummers' cavorting. In each instance, a group of men made the rounds from house to house, expecting at each stop to receive some type of reward for their efforts. And in each instance, there were occasions when the visitors were not welcome. Howe's description of the wayward callers parallels Samuel Breck's account of the mummers' intrusion. Breck, however, recalled an event from the late 1700s, more than a half-century before the demise of the callings that Howe described. The shift in attitude during the time between the two events is remarkable. Although he regarded them as "vagabonds" whose "filthy clothes" were clearly unsuited to the "rich furniture" in the prosperous homes they molested, Breck saw no recourse but to allow the mummers entry. "Custom" had decreed it—a custom of personal obligation and proper behavior that permeated social interaction in the eighteenth century. By the mid-1800s, the rules of social engagement had changed. People belonging to different social groups or classes increasingly lived apart from one another, and casual interaction was not encouraged. By that time the middle-class ideal of the home as a sanctuary was paramount. Charitable obligations were addressed through established aid societies not via handouts at one's own threshold. Better to end a cherished holiday custom than to permit a violation of domestic sanctity.

During the same time period that New Year's Day reigned as the high point of the winter social season, Twelfth Night held the distinction of marking the culmination of the festivities; on January 6, the Feast of the Epiphany, the last formal entertainment occurred. The parties typically were family gatherings in which people of all ages participated. Central to the festivities was the cutting of the Twelfth Night cake, which might be a rich fruit cake. Nicholas Cresswell participated in a Twelfth Night party in Alexandria, Virginia, in 1775:

> Last night I went to the Ball. It seems this is one of their annual Balls supported in the following manner: A large rich cake is provided and cut into small pieces and handed round to the company, who at the same time draws a ticket out of a Hat with something merry wrote on it. He that draws the King has the Honor of treating the company with a Ball the next year, which generally costs him Six or Seven Pounds. The Lady that draws the Queen has the trouble of making the cake.

Guests at a Twelfth Night party could be called upon by the king and queen to sing,

Twelfth Night Cake
Martha Washington's recipe for a "Great Cake," such as would be served on Twelfth Night, lists among the ingredients four pounds each of butter and sugar, five pounds each of flour and fruit, and more than three dozen eggs.

dance, recite, or do anything that might contribute to the fun of the evening. The celebration was especially popular in the Middle Colonies and the South, where Twelfth Day was also a favorite time for weddings. George and Martha Washington were among those who celebrated their wedding anniversary on January 6. In New England, where Puritan influence lingered, the holiday was not so well known.

A different twist on the Twelfth Night observance took place in New Orleans, where many residents were of French descent. There, January 6 marked the occasion of the "King's Ball," inaugurating a round of festivities that continued until the start of the Lenten season. Each week, a new pair of monarchs was crowned at successive balls. In a manner similar to the tradition Nicholas Cresswell observed in Virginia in 1775, a king was chosen via the chance discovery of a bean hidden in a cake. Whomever received the slice with the bean was crowned king or queen; then a consort was chosen from among the assembled company. They reigned for one week, until the next event. Often the balls were masquerades; partygoers were asked to disguise themselves and to act out the role appropriate to their attire. In New Orleans, Twelfth Night festivities are still a milestone. Elsewhere in America, the popularity of Twelfth Night parties waned after 1860. In an increasingly industrial economy, the holidays could not be allowed to stretch for twelve days, from Christmas to Epiphany.

Today Twelfth Night celebrations are all but unknown to most Americans, and New

Year's Day takes a backseat to
Christmas. Another early
American holiday, however, is
still widely celebrated.
Historians continue to debate
when the first Thanksgiving
observance occurred in New
England, but it is known that
throughout the seventeenth
century, clergy or public offi-
cials periodically proclaimed
days for giving thanks in
response to specific events. By the eighteenth
century, a day was regularly set aside in late
November or early December to celebrate the
harvest. Following America's separation from
Great Britain, a national day of thanksgiving
was occasionally proclaimed by government
leaders in response to national initiatives, such
as the ratification of the Constitution or the
end of the War of 1812. It was Abraham
Lincoln who in 1863 instituted the last
Thursday in November as a regularly observed
national holiday; the date was further solidi-
fied when Franklin D. Roosevelt mandated
the fourth Thursday of the month, as we celebrate today.

Other winter holidays that are remem-
bered by modern Americans as relics from
their European ancestors were actually popularized by descendants of those individuals in
America. A classic example is the commemo-
ration of St. Nicholas Day, or December 6, by
people of Dutch ancestry. Celebrated in the
Netherlands as the day when the patron saint
of children arrived to bestow his tokens upon

25

Giving Thanks

A new vegetable accompanied
the roast goose on a 1779
New England Thankgiving table:
"It is called Sellery & you eat it
without cooking."

the good children in each household, there is little to indicate that the Catholic saint's day was observed by the Dutch Reformed settlers of New York prior to the early 1800s. The spur to its popularization began in 1810, when members of the recently organized New-York Historical Society chose to celebrate their organization's anniversary on St. Nicholas Day "in compliment to the original settlers of this State." Among the society's members were two men who through their literary efforts found their names forever linked with St. Nicholas: Washington Irving, whose satirical, pseudo-historical accounts of life in old New York include numerous references to the Dutch gift-giver; and Clement Moore, whose poem "A Visit from St. Nicholas" popularized many of the attributes of the modern Santa Claus. With their colleagues in the historical society, these two so promoted the St. Nicholas legend that they revived observance of the saint's day among some Americans of Dutch descent.

Among the various winter celebrations that have been interpreted on the Yuletide tour, the one with the most ancient origins is the Jewish observance of Hanukkah—the eight-day festival commemorating the rededi-cation of the Temple in Jerusalem after its recovery from the Syrians some two thousand years ago. Wherever Jews have observed Hanukkah, inevitably, the celebrations have come to reflect the ways in which they have interacted with other cultures. For example, although all Jews who celebrate Hanukkah eat special foods cooked in oil at that time, the foods differ depending on the region in which the people reside. In spite of the diversity of the Jewish experience, many of the traditions survive virtually intact. The ritual objects associated with Hanukkah have remained essentially the same. An eight-armed candelabrum called a menorah is lit over eight successive days, with one more candle added to the sequence each day. A top called a dreidel is used by children playing a put-and-take game, but its Hebraic symbols also convey the message of the miracle of the Temple's restoration. The special foods cooked in oil recall the legend that an insufficient supply of oil miraculously kept the Eternal Light burning for eight days. These components of the holiday have remained unchanged.

Specific holiday traditions such as those described, whether observed by the majority of Americans in the past or claimed only by a few, make up the loose framework around which Yuletide at Winterthur revolves. However, the overall scope of the tour is broader, incorporating all the special events that marked the winter social season in the pre-1860 time period. For those individuals who strictly adhered to sanctions against holiday celebrations, the season still presented many opportunities for socializing. Quilting frolics, wedding celebrations, musicales, teas, card parties, elegant balls, and tavern dances have all been depicted on the Yuletide tour at various times. Each provides a tantalizing glimpse of the values and lifestyles of Americans in the preindustrial past.

A Hanukkah Evening

During Hanukkah the ritual candelabrum, or menorah, traditionally has been placed in the window for all to see. Its early use is evidenced in a print by Moritz Oppenheim dating to the late 1800s.

*T*he origins of Yuletide at Winterthur can actually be found decades before the first public tour in 1978. An editorial in the December 19, 1956, issue of the *Winterthur Newsletter* observed that

> during the Holiday Season, anyone at Winterthur might naturally find himself quite aware of the number of posset pots, caudle cups, tankards, tea sets, and other pieces of early American equipment for carrying on the fine art of entertaining. Not only the equipment for eating and drinking, but also the furniture itself often bespeaks provision for the entertainment of guests . . . What was served on those dining tables? What went into the caudle cups and posset pots? What was served on the card and gaming tables? What books were at hand for guests to read? What special celebrations were in the home at Christmas time or any other holiday? Here indeed is ground for further research.

Over the years, subsequent issues of the *Winterthur Newsletter* revisited those questions. Articles emphasized the social usage of the various objects seen in the period rooms. Frequently appearing in December issues, the articles sometimes focused specifically on holiday entertainment or the ways in which early American attitudes toward Christmas differed from modern perceptions of the holiday.

Left: Empire Parlor.

Christmas in Odessa

Since the 1960s, festive table settings have been featured during the holidays at Winterthur's Historic Houses of Odessa.

Their appearance coincided with a growing interest in history as told "from the bottom up"—that is, from the perspectives of "ordinary" people, as opposed to that of the political leaders and social elites who were typically the focus of scholarly pursuit. Understanding the ways in which objects were used, including their roles in the celebrations and other events that punctuated the daily calendar of existence, was one way of revealing this history.

By the mid-1960s, Winterthur was peripherally engaged in interpreting holiday customs through annual participation in Christmas in Odessa, a festive house tour in Odessa, Delaware, where Winterthur operates several historic house museums. In 1966 "The Christmas Tree in America" was the theme of a special exhibit at the Corbit-Sharp House there. The following year, rooms in the house were decorated with greens, flowers, and tables arrayed with foods prepared to evoke a holiday dinner in the early 1800s. "Christmas in Odessa," like similar programs in countless historic communities and house museums, addressed the public interest in seeing how people in the past might actually have used the objects that are displayed in museum settings, and it fueled a sense of nostalgia for a holiday perceived as simpler, purer, and more family-oriented than the commercialized and electrified holidays of the present.

It was not until 1971 that a few of the period rooms at Winterthur were first decorated with fruit pyramids, sweets, and sprigs of greens in acknowledgment of the holiday season. Impetus for the decorations came from several sources. First, during the lifetime of Winterthur's founder, Henry Francis du Pont, fresh flowers had graced the rooms of the museum. In December the arrangements often included seasonal greens that added a festive air, and the talented women who created such arrangements were eager to expand the holiday displays. In addition, visitors touring the museum often inquired about how early Americans celebrated Christmas. Finally, scholars studying the museum's collections of silver, glass, and ceramic tablewares wanted to share information on how these items were used in the past. Their influence is apparent in the early displays, which evoked the elaborate dessert tables enjoyed at fashionable parties in the eighteenth and nineteenth centuries.

The first holiday room settings included three period dining-room displays and a parlor. The parlor was simply decorated with branches of holly placed in existing mantel vases; the addition of a punch bowl and ladle evoked a spirit of conviviality. In the dining rooms, dishes were filled with sweetmeats, and plates were piled high with pyramids of cakes and fruit set off by touches of greenery. The special displays were not advertised but were delightful surprises for visitors to discover as they toured the museum in December.

31

Reflections of Yuletides Past

Prior to the 1800s, few evergreen decorations were used in the home. A filled punch bowl added an air of festivity.

Festive Touches

This English print, *Settling the Affairs of the Nation* (ca. 1800), documents the customs of a "kissing ball" of greens hanging from the ceiling and individual sprigs of greenery embellishing the window panes.

Winterthur's early holiday displays reflected a conscious effort to use objects already in the rooms. Dining rooms naturally lent themselves to displays centered on dessert customs. Few items were added or removed; rather, objects that "lived" in the spaces were rearranged and augmented with a few carefully chosen additions. Apparent today is the fact that there is little one might consider "Christmas-y" about the early displays. Historically, such lavish table settings might have occurred at any time during the year; only the use of holly in one room readily brings Christmas to mind. In fact, the elaborate food displays were not based upon actual Christmas celebrations but were borrowed from images in seventeenth- and eighteenth-century European prints, cookbooks, and encyclopedias. Only one of these specifically alluded to Christmas. As was noted in the *Winterthur Newsletter,* "The four rooms . . . are decorated for an eighteenth-century party rather than decked with Christmas finery because this season in seventeenth- and early eighteenth-century America was usually marked by 'business as usual,' reflecting the Puritan protest against religious ritual and pagan rites."

For several years, the same displays were repeated with only minor changes, but when the Winterthur Guild (the museum's membership branch) was organized in 1976, holiday programs for members became annual events. The next year, a series of festive, members-only December evenings included candle-light tours. Six rooms were featured, specifically four dining rooms, a tavern setting, and a parlor from a Pennsylvania German farmhouse. The tavern setting borrowed its use of boxwood decorations from an English print. Only the farmhouse display took its inspiration from an American source: the tabletop tree was adapted from the 1812 John Lewis Krimmel sketch.

Because of the popularity of the December evening programs for members, in 1978 the number of decorated rooms increased to twelve, and a special tour that focused solely on the holiday settings was introduced to the public. Included was an elegant table setting in the Du Pont Dining Room, with live fruit trees in the centerpiece, and another table in the Queen Anne Dining Room that featured the ever-popular fruit pyramids. The new tour received considerable fanfare. A December 17, 1978, Wilmington *Sunday News Journal* article, "Winterthur Christmas: Splendor of the Past," complete with color photographs, heralded its inauguration. Another feature in the December 1978 issue of *House and Garden* magazine brought the tour to a national audience.

A Pennsylvania German Christmas

Adapted from an 1812 sketch by John Lewis Krimmel (shown on page 13), this tree is decorated with edible treats and a pastoral scene within a fence around the base—the precursor to the electric train encircling the tree.

Deck the Halls

The earliest references to decorating a home with ropes of evergreen date to the 1800s.

Encouraged by the success of the pilot effort, organizers of the holiday program expanded it the following year. More than 12,000 visitors enjoyed touring the fifteen rooms that constituted Yuletide at Winterthur 1979. One of Yuletide's signature displays was introduced that year: the elegant Montmorenci Stair Hall swagged in evergreens, with pots of Jerusalem cherries lining the stairs. Some variation on this display has been included on every subsequent Yuletide tour. Other new exhibits included an early 1820s evening musicale in the Empire Parlor and a late eighteenth-century plantation ball supper in the Marlboro Room. Already home to a harp and a piano, the Empire Parlor easily lent itself to its new interpretation. The Marlboro Room, on the other hand, had to be emptied of most of its furnishings to make room for dancing, as would have been done in the eighteenth century. Such a dramatic transformation of a space was a departure from the earlier practice of adding accessories and foods to otherwise intact displays. It foreshadowed a later imperative to make the room settings more historically correct, with the proper type and quantity of furnishings and accessories for the event and time period depicted.

Among the additions to the Marlboro Room were a number of dishes and glasses that held some remarkable new food displays: colorful composition custards topped with tempting dollops of plaster-of-paris whipped cream and a quantity of that essential period delicacy—rubber oysters on the half-shell. These were Yuletide's first foray into the world of museum-safe faux foods, a field with which tour coordinators were destined to become well acquainted. Although some artificial food was used, most of the delicacies featured on the tour were still fresh, and creating the displays took enormous effort. About fifty museum guides baked the cakes, cookies, pies, and breads and painstakingly created dazzling pyramids by securing countless grapes, apples, and boxwood sprigs to styrofoam cones using toothpicks. Every night the fresh foods were carted to cold storage areas, but most had to be replaced at least once during the holiday season.

Faux Food

Oysters, an expensive delicacy in Europe, were abundant in America. They were served stewed, fried, pickled, and raw.

The challenges presented by having so much fresh food in the period rooms were compounded in 1980 when the tour expanded to twenty rooms and the curators decided to move beyond dessert tables to depict entire meals. This decision resulted in a few years when freeze-dried meats figured prominently in the displays. Prepared months in advance, the meats were packed in dry ice and transported to the Smithsonian Institution in Washington, D.C., where the freeze-drying process had been perfected. The new inclusions were dramatic: pheasants, geese, and a

36

Holiday Feasts

The winter season was a time for feasting on recently harvested vegetables and freshly butchered meats.

whole roasted pig. They served the museum well for several years, until the unfortunate discovery that freeze-dried fish placed too close to freshly baked Johnny cakes would rehydrate, with predictable results.

As the tour grew both in scope and popularity, its emphasis on historical accuracy increased. Reliance upon European sources diminished as ongoing research resulted in greater familiarity with holiday customs, entertainments, and foodways in America. Greater attention was given to the details of each room display to make sure that all the objects included could reasonably have been there in the time period being interpreted. The challenges inherent in designing a holiday tour around the 1640–1860 time frame of the Winterthur collection—a period when many of our holiday "traditions" did not exist—meant that particular effort had to be given to controlling any impulses to romanticize the past. Recognizing that the tour is "an extension of our program to increase understanding of American culture," tour directors and curators "tried to curb our imagination and document the food, plant material, and other objects that relate to the theme of the tour."

In subsequent years, new twists in the

holiday celebrations were portrayed on tour, including several displays that recounted how Henry Francis du Pont and his family celebrated Christmas and New Year's Day when they resided at Winterthur. Included were rooms depicting a Christmas Day luncheon, with food, flowers, tablewares, and decorations replicated from archival lists; an eighteen-foot Christmas tree in the Conservatory; and a New Year's Day calling. By 1985 more than 20,000 people incorporated Yuletide at Winterthur into their holiday celebrations. That year one of the tour's most enduring displays originated: a magnificent tree in the Conservatory embellished with a multitude of white lights illuminating an abundant array of exquisite dried flowers.

Early Winterthur holiday displays focused primarily on traditions brought to this country by émigrés from England and Germany, with occasional references to the French and the Dutch. The rooms emphasized Christmas, New Year's Day, and Twelfth Night. More recently, interpreting alternative viewpoints and the experiences of people in disparate life situations has been a goal. Since a significant number of Americans prior to

Christmas at Winterthur

When Henry Francis du Pont resided at Winterthur, Christmas gifts for each family member were placed in large baskets under the tree in the Conservatory and brought inside for the gift exchange on Christmas Day.

Homage to the Winterthur Garden

This breathtakingly beautiful display in the Conservatory remained a tour highlight for many years. Many of the dried flowers come from the Winterthur Garden.

1860 opposed celebrating Christmas on religious grounds, the Yuletide tour has also included vignettes that evoke the quiet non-observance of the Quakers and people belonging to other nonconformist sects. Other displays have featured the frequent, though not always happy, interaction between masters and servants, rich and poor, devout and secular, and others who often had widely different opinions as to how the holidays should properly be observed. Such efforts present a broader representation of the winter experiences of people from diverse ethnic, racial, and socioeconomic circumstances as well as the elites of society, whose festive tables were evoked by the earliest Yuletide displays.

Along with new interpretive topics, with the late 1980s came a host of new display techniques intended to help bring the exhibits to life. Adding a blanket of sparkling snow and glistening icicles to the Court transformed that already-magical space into a dazzling wonderland. Carolers singing tunes specially chosen and recorded for Winterthur contributed to the impact. From music, the inclusion of specially recorded sound effects to evoke a Christmas morning foxhunt at George Washington's Mount Vernon or the boisterousness of youths carousing through the streets on New Year's Day was a logical step. At various times, dummyboards—predecessors of the two-dimensional lawn figures seen today—populated some of the rooms as they did in the eighteenth century. Mannequins serve the same purpose while providing a vehicle to display period costumes. Camera techniques have ranged from still shots that are projected onto a screen to replicate a magic lantern show to Disney-inspired holograms that fill a room with ghost-like dancers.

All these techniques have been effective at capturing the imagination of museum visitors. More subtle, but no less effective,

Let it Snow!

The interior Courtyard is transformed to a winter wonderland for Yuletide.

have been advances made in the area of artificial foods. The use of real foods in the museum has always been problematic. For example, prior to 1987, the "wine" included in many of the room displays was actually a colored liquid. Although not truly wine, it did threaten damage to the collection should it be spilled. That danger was averted through the talents of a local chemist, who filled reproduction glasses with epoxy wine that are still in use today. One year a display of pies cooling on a dresser proved too tempting for a visitor passing by. He simply did not believe that the crusts were real—until he put his hand through one. Real foods were fragile and deteriorated over time, and some had to be replaced several times during the run of the tour. Because of these and other problems associated with their use, in 1993 real foods were permanently banned from the period rooms. This presented a challenge, for over the years the Yuletide storage areas had accumulated an abundance of special sweets. Rock hard, they still looked fabulous. It was

Baker's Delight

A tempting 1830s dessert table features genuine cakes and cookies made in the traditional manner.

Just Desserts

This 1830s dessert table features sweets made of papier-mâché, plaster of paris, paraffin, styrofoam, and spackle.

an uneasy day when the closets were purged of all the fancy cakes, colorful marzipans, and pristine white meringues that were Yuletide's stock-in-trade.

A search for suitable replacements for the lost sweets and other new additions led first to suppliers of faux foods for restaurant displays. While their products were of high quality, their large fruits and plump fowl were not historically correct. They were clearly reflections of late twentieth-century ideals. In the end, just as it was the Winterthur guides who supplied the real baked goods for the early displays, talented members of the education staff have produced their faux descendants in later years. Their efforts begin, as always, with research, which often means preparing an actual dish from a historical recipe to see how it looks—and tastes!—so that it may be accurately replicated. As experience accumulated, new media were introduced, and progressively more realistic foods have resulted; the line has expanded to include fruits, vegetables, and meats. Winterthur's food artists have even had the opportunity to share their secrets for making museum-safe faux foods with colleagues at workshops held across the country.

All the research and all the display techniques that have been incorporated into Yuletide at Winterthur during the past two decades have resulted in a tour that in recent years has averaged an annual attendance of about 27,000 visitors. Many write to express both their surprise and their delight at what they have experienced on the tour. They thank us for giving them a sense of the rich history of the holiday season, for helping them to see where the customs they hold dear originated, for reviving traditions of their youth that have been forgotten with the passage of time, and for creating new memories and new traditions to share with their families. Over the years, as Yuletide at Winterthur has attempted to reveal the holiday traditions enjoyed by our ancestors, it has itself become a tradition, something that people return to year after year and cherish as part of their holiday ritual. In turn, they share with us their own traditions, stories, and memories of holidays past. In doing so, they bring new meaning to the objects on display, infuse new life into the museum rooms, and invoke the spirit of the holiday season in a way that enriches us all.

41

Christmas Cookies
German settlers of Pennsylvania in the early 1800s decorated their windows with cookies.

An outdoor tree decorated with edible ornaments provides a Yuletide treat for Winterthur's wildlife.

1966   "The Christmas Tree in America" is the theme of an exhibit at Winterthur's Historic Houses of Odessa.

1971   Four rooms at Winterthur are decorated with greens and festive fare as a surprise for visitors taking December tours.

1977   The first holiday evening program is held for members of the Winterthur Guild.

1978   A tour including specially decorated rooms is available to museum visitors. Approximately 1,200 people participate.

1979   The public holiday program, now called Yuletide at Winterthur, expands in length and capacity to accommodate more than 12,000 visitors.

        Montmorenci Stair Hall is decorated with swagging and pots of Jerusalem cherries.

        The first custom faux foods are introduced.

1980   *Yuletide at Winterthur: Tastes and Visions of the Season* is published.

        Freeze-dried foods are introduced.

1982   The first displays depicting holiday customs of Henry Francis du Pont appear on the Yuletide tour.

1983   Former Winterthur curator Louise Conway Belden publishes *The Festive Tradition: Table Decoration and Desserts in America, 1650–1900.*

1985   An eighteen-foot tree decorated with white lights and dried flowers adorns the Conservatory.

        More than 20,000 visitors enjoy Yuletide at Winterthur.

1993   Real foods in all forms are banned from the period rooms.

1997   Winterthur hosts the Mid-Atlantic Association of Museums at a conference devoted to creating museum-safe faux foods.

        More than 26,800 people participate in Yuletide at Winterthur.

To learn more about the site of some of the earliest Winterthur-related holiday tours, see *Discover the Historic Houses of Odessa* by Steven M. Pulinka and Deborah N. Buckson.